DUCK
EATS
YEAST,
QUACKS,
EXPLODES;
MAN
LOSES
EYE

a poem

ESSENTIAL POETS SERIES 301

Guernica Editions Inc. acknowledges the support of
the Canada Council for the Arts and the Ontario Arts Council.
The Ontario Arts Council is an agency of the Government of Ontario.

We acknowledge the financial support of the Government of Canada

Gary Barwin
& Lillian Nećakov

DUCK
EATS
YEAST,
QUACKS,
EXPLODES;
MAN
LOSES
EYE
a poem

GUERNICA
EDITIONS

TORONTO • CHICAGO • BUFFALO • LANCASTER (U.K.)
2023

Guernica Founder: Antonio D'Alfonso

Michael Mirolla, editor
Cover and Interior Design: Rafael Chimicatti
Front cover image: Gary Barwin
Guernica Editions Inc.
287 Templemead Drive, Hamilton (ON), Canada L8W 2W4
2250 Military Road, Tonawanda, N.Y. 14150-6000 U.S.A.
www.guernicaeditions.com

Distributors:
Independent Publishers Group (IPG)
600 North Pulaski Road, Chicago IL 60624
University of Toronto Press Distribution (UTP)
5201 Dufferin Street, Toronto (ON), Canada M3H 5T8
Gazelle Book Services
White Cross Mills, High Town, Lancaster LA1 4XS U.K.

First edition.
Printed in Canada.

Legal Deposit – First Quarter
Library of Congress Catalog Card Number: 2022945566
Library and Archives Canada Cataloguing in Publication
Title: Duck eats yeast, quacks, explodes; man loses eye : a poem / Gary Barwin
& Lillian Nećakov.
Names: Barwin, Gary, author. | Nećakov, Lillian, 1960- author.
Series: Essential poets ; 301.
Description: Series statement: Essential poets series ; 301
Identifiers: Canadiana 20220419574 | ISBN 9781771837811 (softcover)
Classification: LCC PS8553.A783 D83 2023 | DDC C811/.54—dc23

DUCK EATS YEAST, QUACKS, EXPLODES; MAN LOSES EYE

Rhadamanthus's Unusually Fermented Sunday Breakfast Causes It to Rise Piecemeal, Blinding Owner.

DES MOINES, Ia., Jan. 2 – The strangest accident recorded in local history occurred this morning when Rhadamanthus, a duck, which took a prize at the recent Iowa poultry show, exploded into several hundred pieces, one of which struck Silas Perkins in the eye, destroying the sight.

The cause of the explosion was the eating of yeast which was placed in a pan upon the back porch, and tempted his duckship, which was taking a Sunday morning stroll.

Upon returning from church Mr. Perkins discovered his prize duck in a somewhat logy condition. Telltale marks around the pan of yeast gave him his clew.

He was about to pick up the bird when the latter quacked and exploded with a loud report and Mr. Perkins ran into the house holding both hands over one eye. A surgeon was called, who found that the eyeball had been penetrated by a fragment of flying duck and gave no hope of saving the optic.

1

we fly but have not yet arrived
a suspended moment
the possible one
of the provinces of truth
it's delightful

what you say, you say as a duck
you can say nothing outside of this
let us now consider the other eye

2

if we consider the other eye
a small balloon filled with awakening

if the duck's beak splintered into a thousand
truths on which to impale our enemy

3

we drown in what isn't
there light or air

if I were a duck and also king if were
a duck and also lawn furniture
if I were able to be more than one thing

infinite but mortal
sorrow filled with workers
a cliff, neglected
my mother but also my daughter

here take
this eye

4

if I look upon
the whole meadow as an elucidation

as a daughter looks for her lost mother among the discarded life nets
tangled in the sea
of a duck's dream

if with this gift I move big waters turn
the heads of smirking clocks way, way back
the earth just a bruise
on the tip of a tongue

5

the world is tender
the tip of a duck's tongue

hush

we swim through the present bruise

the neck of a mallard
the iridescent neck of a duck
the underside of stone

hush

in the pond the wake needs to lead
in the meadow the gun needs its bayonet
the impossible
one of the provinces of truth

hush

when I returned from church my husband
was missing an eye

6

we searched where the ducks
slept in the pig's embrace

hush said the reeds
hush said the pond
the impossible
a province of its own

hush

bayonet-faced wife your husband will swim
back to you

on the back of a mallard on the back of a stone

hush

small husband
there is so much joy
in the sorrow of a king

7

what explodes?
the duck, obviously
but also

springtime
our downy heart
duckling size

here our small husband a soldier
stands in the palm of our right hand

a duck eats yeast
explodes
mother runs from the barn
father runs from the kitchen
sun sinks to the horizon
meadow can only flower

the hired man dances
the hired man is dances
hand raised to brow

oh I've lost an eye
lost an eye
I have only feathers now
all I see is sky

8

the horizon spread her downy wings over the wingless and the mute

again the hired man is dances
palms to the sky
to the sky

jig as strong as magic
jig to bring the sun to its knees
jar full of stars

a feathered aria
the hired man is dances

9

another eye another eye another eye a duck a duck a duck another eye

when the yeast rises the sun rises when the sun falls the bread stays tall

is the human heart a duck?
is the poem an eye?
is the cathedral of the future
flame?

10

and the tzadikim and the prophets and
the saints raise their shillelaghs
to the sky

the beasts bow
the husband a tiny blade
on the wife's brow
the yeast grows
and the bread rises

we feel something exploding
a blind eye

11

and if it all unravels

ducks gather
pan fills with yeast
then we too can start
swimming back
through our own wake

we're old and become young
we're tall and become short
the constellation of our bodies
an egg

something happened in Des Moines involving a duck, some yeast, a man
his eye

it's still happening

12

that thing in Des Moines
a reckoning
an unravelling
an affirmation of will

there is no future
in eggs
only springtime
and the incessant
quack quacking
all those goddamn wakes

13

June 1910

he types late into the night Silas Perkins
exceeding limits

let's imagine everything inside
the curling dark of a nautilus snail

springtime
springtime
springtime

inside these words

14

the joys of June follow
the narrator spirals
the galaxy of the cephalopod's fold

forgetting
why should we remember?
war of the eyes
the planets and the churches
the cigars of his sophomoric youth

why should spring
the snail it is
echo back balmy
nights when the presses ran
night and day

we sat in Silas Perkins' park
around small fires that burn
the hearts of our kin
to ash

15

let snail be n
the eye's long view a
for it is a soft planet x

let our words be p and h
our joy Q
Σ its axial tilt
you Φ and I Φ
the spiral turn of galaxy Δ always

$$(x + p)^n = \sum_{h=0}^{n} \left(\frac{n}{Q}\right) x^{\Phi} a^{n-\Delta}$$

we solved puzzles
Silas whittling
a thousand years from now
our shadow intimate as ducks

16

if we take for example Mos Def's mathematics beats by Su-Primo
even numbers have limits these firecrackers being
off-limits

then suppose a Shakespearian sonnet
in Euler's hand
$e^{i\pi} + 1 = 0$
numbers still have fences

a thousand whittled sticks
the one constant
while outside remains
∵ the field waddles, tilts $\dfrac{\pi}{2}$

and you are still Ω and I am still Ω numbers have limits
and Silas got limits
the ducks got limits

17

I recall answers
but not questions

Please put it on my bill
because it's too far to waddle
because they grow down
n+127
firequackers

there in the dust
we say nothing
a cradle for loud

take a poem
wait

what happens?
love?

poem as entropic story
grammar's big band
dark matter clarinet
accordion
a mathematics of breath

my theory is
the universe is
tender and murderous

you know those things
that hold up the sleeves of
an old timey newspaperman—
a sleeve garter?
the universe is a sleeve garter

clarinet accordion cephalopod
and oh $e^{i\pi} + 1 = 0$
bones above the naked hand
Harmon mute
velvet handkerchief

18

but the question *is*
the answer

just before the gloaming
before buttery stars
straddle the sky

we exist to grieve
a theory of a cosmos expanded
a geometry of ivory

although the Milky Way is frail
storied
there *are* bands of gunpowder grey

there *are* entropic molecules
fused to firecrackers
there *are* ducks and envy
there *are* sleeves
worn in answer

20

so, now that the yeast
        and the duck and cook have exploded
        the eye
and the husband
the bayonet-faced wife
and Silas have gone back into the church
the mathematicians
and the accordions
the poets
and the snails have all been furloughed
we return to the beginning

the duck
the yeast
the eye

21

we arrive at parody though
present is always
a parody of past
and past
of present

hope is hope with a mask on
just as we grieve time

a forest writes with trees
an ocean with water
and we

written

22

how we arrive
for example in the shape of
an ocean in the shape of
a parallelogram, a tree

ah, and we return
to holy ones
as if by knife

the paradigm shifts
and the duck is now
quiet as x

23

the duck
the yeast
the eye

hush =

history

over the wheat field
where Silas Perkins was born

he raises a hand it contains an eye
he raises a barn it contains a duckling
he raises four daughters

a parallelogram of daughters in an ocean of trees
a paradox of trees around an ocean of daughters
the bayonet of night pierces stars

hush =

hush =

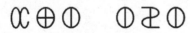

eye - eye (open)
-y- - -y- (closed)

ocean no larger than x

24

there is a lung
< hush
a big bang

a planet, Silas
3 ducks and a daughter
a narrator
always a narrator

when one eye opens
another closes

when the narrator
stops narrating
the bread rises

25

somewhere in another poem
not this one
something else

wolf folds up forest
steps out of the tale
the underside of road is still road

a soldier parts war
like a curtain
lays naked on the floor

a lung and its other
leave the body
vultures filled with air

birds are where birdholes are not
but what about the birds that
are not?

26

‖‖‖
‖‖‖

birdholes stuffed with

‖‖‖
‖‖‖

soldiers
along a road
ripped raw
by the wolf

single lungs lost
in another poem
vulturing around
for their mate

ten ways to skin
each flake of snow

27

how many days until
we're far from now

卌

new fallen skin
susceptible to bootprints

卌

the body a cave
bullet holes
what isn't snow

卌

throat a bird hole
where there once was song

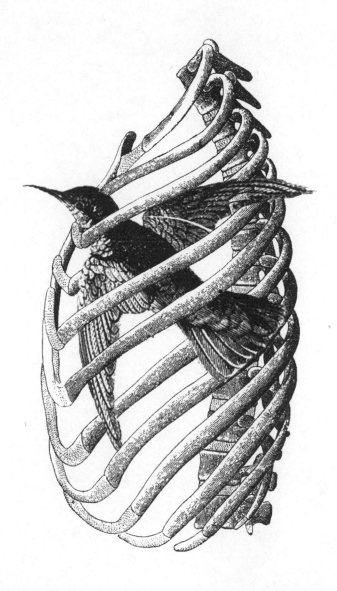

ab cd ef gh ij kl mn
op qr st uv wx yz

hollow as a ribcage
a breath from home

(if the alphabet were lungs)
thirteen soldiers

perforated stars
unlocked the war

ribs window
light as whip stripes
language unable

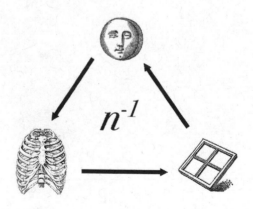

$$n^{-1}$$

А Б В Г Д Ђ Е Ж З И Ј К Л Љ М Н Њ О П Р С Т Ћ У Ф Х Ц

3 soldiers missing

31

hush > somewhere there's a farm
in a sick bed
put your ear to bullet holes
put your ear to the chest
a perforated tin lantern
listen through bullet holes
breath illuminating stars
birds see their own shadow as they fly

hush > a soldier asks
what makes snow out of rain
a soldier in a field remains rain
a soldier in a field reminds rain
rain becomes river the soldier wades
the river of his own death

hush > the sergeant says
you can't wade into the same death twice
not if it's your own

hush > три војника нестала
a thousand thousand snowflakes
a single hand above the snow
a soldier in a field remains rain

what did we do when it rained

hush

32

a skylark circles
in witness
seamlessly
a taxidermist
the sergeant skins
shadow after shadow

earth shudders

hush
whispers
god
it's all part
of
simple
mathematics

33

in sleep the taxidermist
climbs out of himself
skin shadow

bed a skylark
sleep a skylark
brainlobe wings
waves

his skinless body
bones, flesh
soldiers sunk below
the seam
scars sunk beneath witness

hush > listen
to the tiny rumble
each letter
a quivering against b
b against c
c and d quaking together and so to z
alphabet
an inkblack spiral

34

where in all this is the funeral?
the bustling bodies pressed
b to d
(body to death)
prayer to lip
death to death
where are the seamstresses
to stitch back this gaping hole
of
and
alphabet
gone

35

ask the birds to forgive us

      the skylarks
      the swallows, the starlings
      the swans, the hawks, the jays
      the emus, the ostriches, the geese
      ask the ducks to forgive us

ask the soldiers, the alphabet
the dirt, ask mathematics always needing more
and less
ask our speechless eyes
to forgive

our mouths, another language in this language
part it like a wound

36

if a if b
if bird if soldier
if wound if word
if hush if shout
if eye scar
sky sleep
if number if limb
bed ladder
child if war
river if meadow

one hand
less than six fingers
more than four

less than six fingers
more than four
on the other

less than two mouths
more than none

less than two lives
more than never having been born

song this grief
this boy this happiness
this joy this girl
sorrow sadness
mountain skylark
this ocean this tongue
dark this beginning
story this end

St. Augustine says
we should not start at the beginning
nor the end
but where we are, in the middle

37

St. Augustine the forager
begins
too late have I loved you

gathers the sixth
the fourth
the second the naught

alpha the zed
the ocean's tongue
bird's soldier

shadow
infinitude
meadow's ladder
the boy's snow

St. Augustine
the skylark
plucks pear after pear
not the first not the last

a sorrow
an ocean
a life x a life x a life

38

when Chewbacca starts shaving
where does he begin?

Nel mezzo del cammin di nostra vita
in the middle of
the middle one the possible provinces of truth

something we were saying
or that was being said
an alphabet whose a seems infinitely distant
whose z does, too

life, a theory
)   (

being born is an erasure
of what isn't us

alpha bravo charlie
St Augustine
they called him
in the middle of an ocean

in big band theory
second trumpeter is king

39

it begins with the typewriter ribbon
Möbius strip imprinted with
Charlie Parker
a trumpeter swan
a middle eight
followed by a crescendo

a fall from grace
but only mezzo
m and *n* mnemonic
down the hatch

ocean flowing backward
the middle of what you were
saying
and what I was not
(   )

40

Bird on a mountain in a swan-white suit
Benny in the sky
dark as shadow, clarinets
Dizzy rising from underwater
Benny + Bird +Diz
wave + wave + wave

what would it be
buried in words
what would it look like
the other side of saying

41

... .. .-... . -. -.-. .

how the quiescence weaves
a hole in the heart
of the dizzy bird
... .. .-... . -. -.-. .

how silent we are when
in the mouth of a howl
... .. .-... . -. -.-. .

how a wave weaves
into a hurricane
... .. .-... . -. -.-. .

how arrogantly the day
wanes

... .. .-.. . -. -.-. .

А Б В Г Д Ђ Е Ж З И Ј К Л Љ М Н Њ О П Р С Т Ћ У Ф Х Ц

卌

hush

how many bones in the human body
a syllabary of possible fracture

owl the word for owl to another owl
night no word for itself
is always surprised when it is gone

is there language without language
body without body

there's a great joke the moon tells when it is covered by cloud
what is it?
don't know
it's covered by cloud

cloud is the rib cage holding in
the moon and the moon's joke

phalanges, prisoners

(

clavicle, the wave that is not
wave that is owl

vertebrae, runes eroding
½ then ¼ then days

y the body is a footnote
to the wisecracking cosmos

x the janitor
eraser and mop in hand

44

inside the body
a forest of nerves
arteries, veins
columns of bone
Greek ruins

in the broom closet
Old Mr Jones, heart
and janitor

| || ||| |||| |||||

Old Mr Jones
thump thump
working until
death like an owl

hush

Old Mr Jones reading this poem
lost his copy

after 1000 years
an owl flew onto the headstone
the poem its mouth
"a miracle!" Old Mr Jones thumped
"not really," the owl said
"your name's written all over it"

45

body makes its mark
thousands of days
stops to count each brand of thump

the forest of nerves grows
into a mouth
that cannot contain
the poem

the broom forgets it is a broom
remembers it was once a small pile
of nerves

lost name
finds its bag of skin

46

days count themselves in clouds
an owl inside Mr Jones
Mr Jones inside that owl
inside that
a cloud
downy as heart

> > > >

nerves are rain
blood bites air so we can survive
not when we're buried but
always
our mantle of air
the blue lining that is our heart

Mr Jones whips off his coat like a cape
flashes the sky-blue lining
scalloped waves, a beating heart

47

no
the blood cannot bite the apple nor the sky nor the blue nor
the wave
can only move through skin like blue to
its lover

48

in the metropolis of the body, blood is a riot

a. what do we want?
    time
    when do we want it?
    how can we know till we get it?
b. we protest government by wound
c. blue is movement
    a wave which blues our brain
                    blurs

                    everything seems/
                    seams

    Hesiod says a bronze anvil falling from heaven would
    fall nine days before it reaches earth

49

we riot against the anvil
between body and want

nine days until we can hold Hesiod's
bull-like earth shaker

shrunken head filled with seeds
blue blue tomorrows

50

I'm 16 and in a stolen car I call
bull-like earth shaker

music blasting
heart like *bull-like earth shaker*

I ride up the mountain
raise fuck-you *earth-shaker* fist
my breath anvil falling

beside *bull-like*
bird exchanges molecules with blue

anger can only be understood backwards
paid forward

sixteen, stealing a bird

the neighbours' pigeon coop
more anger than molecules
little punk-shit unable to math my way out

52

the path from song to *fuck you*
is Möbius

my fist
a shit murmuration

thing + 1 more thing is
1 more fucking thing

$T1 + T2 = fT3$

hardly a bullshit earthshaker but
a formula I know

a crap ton here
but at least it's my crap ton

stars look like meek and sappy twinklers
but they're blazing rioting mindfuckers

53

teetering on this fuckery of a planet
we turn to meek twinklers
for salvation

geometric theory
solid figures composed of vertices
edges, flat faces

all those fucking
fT3

the Möbius strip
twist and shout

54

writhe and shout
bloom and shout
multiply

attach and shout
adore and shout
implore

twinkle and shout
bird and shout
fuck

think and shout
spurt and shout
flower

quiet and shout
squash and shout
piss

sleep and shout
please and shout
age

write and shout
breathe and shout
whisper

moon and shout
tree and shout
riot

shout and

55

(+) + (+) = write and

$O_2 + CO_2$ = breathe and

dark matter of the
the body falling

push and pull
the accordion breathing

time breathing trees
it takes years

but
hey!

we leap
leap!

world falling
to catch us

step with the left
catch the moon

meet left with right
dawn infinite pink

forward with left
larger than cloud

forward with right
ghosts clothed in feeling
leap a coffin, kiss the dead
meet right with left

rain between fingers
forward with right

owls so quiet
hey!

hey hey hey!
catch a sound

shout what was
throw it around

+ + + = +

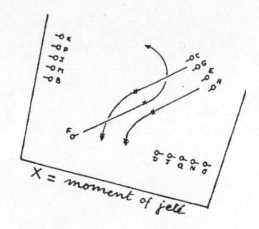

X = moment of jeté

the sound of Fred Astaire's heart
with Ginger

was the left equal to or
greater than the right?

stars or owls

Ginger's jeté
the moon's throat

the intricate
code of Fred's shoes

the ghost equal to or
greater than a world falling

58

the rain sings in us
only have to bathe our outsides

the space between drops
wet

dogs play clavichord
philosophers howl

light only a wave when you take a step back
a star isn't there if you wait long enough

no such thing as bird's eye view
birds don't look down

it's me that's my country

59

the philosophy of country
is bird, human, space, howl

the inside of each drop of rain

       T

an accordion
a violin inside blood

no, wait:
a tuba inside an owl
because tuba-filled life

       T

calculate the poem
e.g. rain the oompah of birds' hearts
a network inside the howl

       $p=i^*n$

solve for philosophy $p=p$

drawing the borders of a poem
means keeping the meaning in

60

an accordion
will not solve for p or x
it will simply get the tuba's
blood boiling

will cause the owl to fly one degree of latitude
west

$$M = 111,132.92 - 559.82 \cos 2\varphi + 1.175 \cos 4\varphi \; 0.00236 \varphi \cos + \ldots$$

the lines of longitude unable to hold her
she will become a human poem
a sine

61

intermezzo

now is the time
Bird said
rich with lowhanging fruit
human comedy
our mitts gripping throat-big sodas
popped corn
each other

now is the time
each-to-each
comedians of blue-black literacy
sines
taken for wonders
the owl in the centre of the mind
a shaggy dog

but said Oscar Wilde
what we hold
we hold close to our chests
the accordion
its wingbeats' low flutter

we bellow our longitudinal polkas
here we are
submerged in unfixed air
our one hit wonder
life together

62

atto due

the shrinking of timetrees
leaves touching down
mid-flight a new schism

the other will stand alone
as the equator

those guilty
plucking each letter off
jagged bone

63

                               O

  w   w   w   w

tree   tree   tree   tree   tree

  Y   Y   Y   Y

alphabet invents humans because
necessary

landscape invents time
invents moon

one wing invents the other
invents bird

bird flies over the landscape
tincanning with other birds

sky invents telephone so
it could

it is precisely at the juncture of d

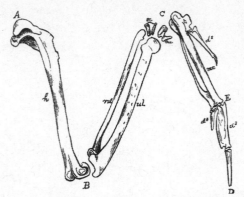

the ambrosial springploof
that the world rumpus
of flight/life begins

at a and the heartcage
that god places
a likeness of her selves

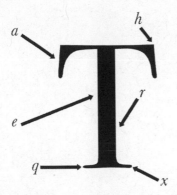

a in the scaphoiddark nectarprose of the azure
proximal flower
you are here

malleus lungs e risking the blue skateboard glorious
beyond all vertibral forestation
you are here

the juncture of h occipital shadows
dowsing their tango of distalcuckoo r
the ribs q cartilaginous in the long subclavian grass
while the x a femursquirrel is
a timpanic theorbo of transverse rumpus

the topography of your life within contested history
a fox within the spinney of body
you are here

it is your geography the compass helps find

the anomaly of a femurish
I am here

the   exponential hair murmurs
in the   kitchen sink
I am also   *here*

the tilt   swagger of geodetic north
geographic   jitterbug
we are here

the chemist   making
lung   shadows in the apothecary
we are here

                                       absolute as

the old brandishes topographic arms
my definition of poetry
or mountains

"femur cuticle illium my hair stands up for something
for a thousand stars making the double inward heelflip
near Ursa minor

yes, my head a dwarf star first noticed by
Ejnar Hertzsprung—thanks Eynar—
and it's near collapse—infinite density, here we come

but everything incredulous and made of matter
has collected in the shining hips & luminous
ulna where earholes are planetary

tilt and swagger, I swashbuckle stars the great belt of
my spine diskbright with Orionlike radiance
a pharmacological skateboard of livid celebration

a mountain made of anticipation,
the fuzzy joy of time
if Barbra Streisand were a pre-Beyoncé

supercluster and her cloned dogs
the fossil glow, why, fellas,
think non-Newtonian quantum way we were

dayglo skylarks escaping the coruscated
cage of a bone-house accordion
spacetime a cab dashing through helium

jazzhands to the molecular upskirt
of life's great pelvis, a bone-bright parade
festooned in the we-are-here flesh

here & now"

68

also the matter of the other dwarves
auch haben klein angefangen
the small crucify the weak
also poetry

Werner's rogue school of thermodynamics

lesson 1: conceptual thinking = digging a hole

lesson 2: the mountain is a river = we are swashbucklers
        = the steamship is a skylark

lesson 3: Delphinus = the dwarves escape to Byzantium

also a hymn

the density of water, whether it can cans or sits
measure the kinetic energy of the skirt's particles
the volcanic eruptions of the filmmaker's loafers
Rosenheim is burning

reading Lorca on the holy mountain
while Franz Liszt breaks his neck
dancing with the jazzhounds
in the here *and* after

69

only the part of the world that doesn't want to be in a poem
should be in a poem

the only thing worse than making rules
is following rules

grammar you're not the lark of me
gramma, you neither

not wrinkles
jazzwrinkles

as clouds are to water
age is to age

let's leave the ship
haul the mountain beneath it

in our swimming pool this morning
two ducks

a paradox
we don't have a pool or ducks

70

the pool we do not have does not
end in a rational number

the grammar of dusk is ducks
over a failed poetry mountain-

the morning outlarks us
we are breaking rules like sticks

71

oh mashed potato clouds of paradise
poetry is dodgeball with angels
gods whip balls at sateen frocks
clonk! an angel plummets
lodges its smooth head in the earth
leaves grow from its feet, trees are born

angels=meaning
gods=words

angels=love
gods=skylarks

angels=hope
gods=

CORNED BEEF SANDWICH

missing last seen corner of Rue de la Bûcherie and Rue Saint-Julien
des Pauvres wearing two slices of rye, a questionable amount
of mustard and a sly smile

---

poetry is a pair o' dice
$1/6 \times 1/6 = 1/36 = 1 \div 36 = 0.0278$
or 2.78 percent
a game of chance
in other words
gods, the wizards of odds
the difficult part is to believe
in the curtain

always an iteration behind the curtain
a cow can stand next to
corned beef

a knight inside a knight's armour inside (( ))
a vestibule inside a vestibule

there's always mashed potato in the paradise of tubers

x   S   S   x x x S
Þe borȝ brittenëd and brent

73

a.

with one hand
            writing

with the other
            disassembling and
            cleaning my ventriloquist dummy

outher my heart will brast
it says in Mallory

the heart inside the vestibule of the chest

        the knight
            the armour
                the castle
                    the story

the green world grows inside the trees

            … (((((( )))))) …

b.

my dummy
Charlie Delta Oracle
lies for me
lies over the ocean
hand a fist in his chest
holding speech

    —Aye did Thril theel ecstasy?
    —he thalues theory thery nuch but
      the attrehension oth the stars
      thills Thril's thrisky, thunny heart with thrills

74

Alpha Zulu Yankee the unnameable

as it says in *Molloy* (
je suis dans la chambre de ma mère
c'est moi qui vis là maintenant
)

ocean flips the writing on its ass
aye, and with all this I remember
the thaumaturgy of Jodorowsky's holiest mountain

75

an ocean
here's how it works:

you stick your hand in the water
the waves do the talking

sound
ocean
sine

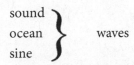

bird flying over ocean
or as bp might wright:

je suis dans la chambre de ma mer
c'est moi qui vis là maintenant

mouth

((( )))

every(((   ))   )thing

every(all at((   ))once)thing

every(all at(toge(   )ther)once)thing

every(all at(toge((((   ))))ther)once)thing

((((((   ))))))

wave

wave

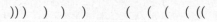

the world forgot to say
what the ocean remembered
the world forgot to say

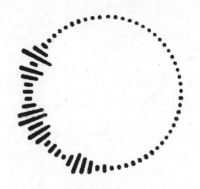

78

let's turn the paren-
theses inside out so that
meaning = everything

)poem(

o
not quite
u

o
pen to sky
u

I cannot change the burden
nothing but the sea

79

if we mean everything the burden is an
O
pen wound

the parentheses the levees

if we mean everything each pin prick
a new constellation
a new
I remember

80

I
remember

would
wound

wound
sound

sound
found

found
song

81

I remember how it all started
not with a wound a sound a song

but with   **;**

duckmoonlarkocean
potatojazzgrammar
bennybirddizdwarf
funeralanvilseamstress

without

    ;

watching from shore
remember

waveoceanoceanoceanocean
oceanwaveoceanoceanocean
oceanoceanwaveoceanocean
oceanoceanoceanwaveocean
oceanoceanoceanoceanwave
oceanoceanoceanoceanocean

windless endless world
a mirror wherein
whales wend below
dive so deep
even unblue is blue

whaleclouds their oceanlark tails undulate under
the secret sun a distant mystery
the bennydizzyjazz of above-light filters
the sea a wound in earth filled with this blue song

whales watched by blue-spanning lark
a sigil a spinning a churning wherein the waves are still

oceananoceananotionamotionanemotionwave
moonanoceantiedbytidebytideashorethewaveashore
waveawaveawareawakeawaveawayawaveawaterawhere

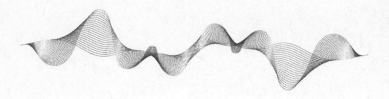

also in the filigree another life as common and elegant {1,2,3,...}

{1,2,3,...}

84

things of the world
countable
uncountable

blue as 1 as 2 as 3
blue as 4 as 5 as 6

what is sky inside lungs
we tree we rock we water

breath as wave
wave as breath

each lung a whale
this dance this 1 this 2
a breath in
breath out
a life a death
flight to the surface
diving down
a beginning an end
an ocean a shore
waves expire
twilight of land where land
yields to water

I sit at the piano to play
Cage's silent piece

I sit at the piano to play
Bach ·

I
wavewhale

a way to become

85

to accommodate the heart
the right whalelung is larger
than the left
a silent film
across the water
230 strands of seagrass
6000 molecules
swaying from left
to right
wave to wave

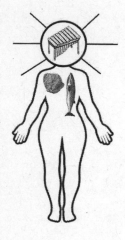

right boulder
left whale
our xylophone smile

instructions in
a musical score:

move through ocean
a baleen whale
with piano-size grin

instructions in
another musical score:

the heart is
a train coming

87

James Baldwin:
write a sentence clean as a bone

o o O O

sometimes sinew
sometimes a train

88

also, James, uh—
Mr Baldwin—
a bone is only clean
not surrounded by body

all the bones
trains
inside sentences
steaming in from somewhere

also, Mr. Frisch, the fog is a body surrounded by another body

a pond that wishes it were a locomotive

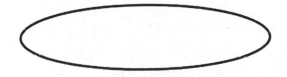

90

the "loneliest whale in the world"
cries for companionship
it sings too high for other whales

most laugh tracks were recorded in 50s
you're laughing with the dead

edgeless ghosts become fog
edgeless frogs become pond

air becomes breath becomes blood
only light when there's a wound

91

we are always laughing with
or *for* the dead
the burden livewires must bear

the body begins to multiply
a bag of laugh explosions
illuminate the wound

92

what people don't know
there are bats in everything

scratch the surface
it's bats

skin over twig bones
laughter swarms

chitters like the dead
once I was walking down King

saw a crack
just past the Italian grocery

bats in the seam
visible for a minute

40 years I've been on high alert
but no bats

once I saw my mother
dead since 1970

93

once I walked *with* King
although I didn't know it

until 40 years later
it was Grafton St. in Dublin

I heard someone yelling
"Seamus Heaney is at Neary's

down the road eating pickled onion
and beetroot in his *going away coat*"

moments later no one was yelling
I walked and walked

bones and cobblestones
knowing what people don't know

buttons in the street
black as beetles

Translations from English

They did not break each other by splitting open in vain[1]

She diminished with respect to her heart[2]

I returned to eat sorrow in my house[3]

After they turn into bats, they shout[4]

[1]My little older sisters fell in their hearts
like carts over cobblestones

[2]We waited all day on the porch while
it rained, but he didn't arrive

[3]He had on his *going away* coat, his *never coming back* face

[4]Bats are twilight if twilight had wings
What do we locate with our keening?
What's behind the surface of the world?
Bats and darkness are behind the surface of the world

95

I am overcome by fatalist geography
= walk the surface of the earth in ancestral shoes

if rain is buckets-full = *the Coney Island of the Mind* is
a soggy-eyed boy

because I am still waiting, not for Godot, but for Ferlinghetti
= a small poem will drop dead in my lap

when I grow wings
my dog will not recognize me = I will always walk alone

those bats and their hearts
rough as cobblestones = the coal man at the door

a new map of the world

what we mean is what we mean + what we don't know
the outside is in everything

the inside is outside everything
we make meaning outside what we mean but mean it anyway

Groucho said dogs see only what is outside them
inside a library it's dark when the books are closed

97

when the books are closed, the dogs, meaning, the alphabet
Groucho, Seamus, time, matter, holiness, the sky, Coney Island

the writer bows her head
so full

98

a list of everything that doesn't exist:

99

and so
to begin

a book

lay down the palm as if on a baby's head
wrap a thumb

turn the palm over
        a gesture "and so?"
        the hand is empty

an opening

everything that exists

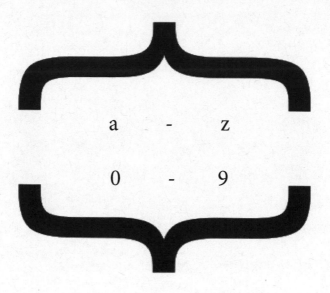

everything that does not

101

I don't exist
yet
here we are
rattling the bars
the fourth

102

the ratio of the circumference of a hug
one arm equals the beauty
of the other arm

holding a body
not in motion
a body
not falling
a body at rest

from 0 to 100
the time it takes to write
everything and nothing

Achilles runs from a to b
then from b to c
the sun tilts in the sky
he runs from c to d then on to e
bees in clover in long grass
long shadows
shepherds yawn in fields

meanwhile the tortoise makes it from
one side of a to the other
what is between a and b?
the tortoise thinks
that inkless stretch?

why the alphabet?
because you are full of rage
why are you full of rage?
because the alphabet

104

a and b pulled from fire
dipped in a river made of sticks
transform into serifless moons
banished from the alphabet
belly to belly

the inkless stretch
Achilles' way

105

a

sky and water move, the ground stays still
then there's an earthquake

b

memory, says Plotinus
is for those who have forgotten

a

to move from a to b means
remembering a

b

gods have no memory because
they don't forget

a

a burned beyond recognition

b

* alpha centauri

                    * beta centauri

* bright stars in the constellation Centaurus
named for Chiron

106

O
yes
son of the sea nymph
released to stipple the night
a thousand glowing boneshards

lighting the way for
alpha to turn to *beta*

stretching oxhide over the olive tree
stretching new vowels

everything the constellations
want us to forget

man erased:
square
circle
drum
frame
shroud
an empty stage
O
son of sea
daughter of land
queer shore
□
humans as
O
mouth
cave
entrance
constellation of stars
O
moon
sun
earth
universe
O
pondripple of space and time
□
alphabet pointing to
what isn't alphabet

108

ᚱᛏᛁᚷᚤᚤ ᛁᚱᚢᚾᚤᛁᛁ ᚾᚤᚤᚷᚤ ᚷᛁᛁᛁᚤ

alphabet-hunters

guided by starripple

O cliffside scarred

the expansion of humankind

hunters of that ripple

109

hunters track / moth gatherers seek
bodyshapes / dayskin

we born we family we sex we scribe
deerwoman / buffaloman

ochre flickerlight
a scar the brain grows around

the body legible / other bodies

110

some susurration of owl
negative capability of the deliberately saxophonic
finger positions of twilight

```
          o
   x      o
          o
            x
          o
          o
          o
     x

          x
   o      x
          x
            o
          x
          x
          x
     x
```

blue-violet and orange-red light
675 nm
chlorophyll b
green light
640 nm

111

Hawkins' birds
schizophrenic around the forest axle

Stan Getzing = Moonlight over Vermont

a mercy
opium sap dawdling in the tree belly

your head's a xylophone, your lungs are a rock and whale
O your head's a xylophone, your lungs are a rock and whale
Baby, I was blue with you always, even when you came unfurled

Yes, Baby blue
Light blue
Periwinkle
Powder blue
Ice blue
Morning blue
Computer web color blue
International Klein Blue
pigment blue
psychological primary blue
Blue (Munsell)
Blue (Pantone)
Blue (Crayola)
Uranium blue
Medium blue
Argentinian blue
Ruddy blue
Savoy blue
Celtic blue
Spanish blue
Liberty blue
Egyptian blue
Ultramarine
Neon blue
Bleu de France

Delft blue
Duck blue
Dark blue
Picotée blue
Resolution blue
Polynesian blue
Navy blue
Midnight blue
Sapphire
Independence
Space cadet
Fluorescent blue
Penn blue
Berkeley blue
Teal

113

I have dipped my dearest's
fingers in the bluesiest blues
from $Fe_4[Fe(CN)_6]_3$
on the shores of the Baltic sea
to the inkwells of
Turnbull's blue

I have sailed the Polynesian seas
under sapphire
hunting for fish and lung
I have been Celt/Spaniard/Egyptian
xylophoned my way across Argentina

I have dipped into the blue ice of morning

114

o love, if you only have blue,
everything is sky

in the frozen river
explain blue to morpho butterfly, corpse

explain blue to a drop of water
to a whale

o love
blood is blue until air

lake doesn't know the secret of its water
running rivers, never the same blue

a blue eye can't see the eye beside it
and you sleep wrapped in bluest blue

blue earth blue sky our love
blue in the palace of ice

lungs blue alphabet, my love
our life, blue mountain shadow, ink

115

o love
o conjoined days
o life that is mountain, my shadow
   whale in the corpse of a river
o blooming lung
   ink lake night
o water from water
   sideways sky
o sleepwalking in whale
o blue-black city lights
   heart laughing turquoise
o bluebell dawn
   motherless light
o e sharp fat F
   fishing with John
o wings
o love
o love
o z

o light from your shank
  whetstone inoculated by sword
o tiretracks
  wattle near wattle
  slash flower
o black clang fingers in the heart
  everyone and no-one crawling from the grapes of the body
o blameless, toothless naked sleep
o letterless John
  mangled shoreline of embrace
o lump
o lump
o breath
o breath
o moon
o

117

yes, Mr Ferlinghetti
Mr Simic is
happy to be a stone
no, Ms. Plath
I have not borrowed
the light
why, Ms. Dickinson
do the whiskers
grow gold?
love is no stone on the moon

118

Yuri Gagarin sad cosmonaut
hands the size of Vostok 1

Belka, Strelka, Laika, Albina
dog teeth clicking like dice

119

Neil Armstrong
outside while his dog pees

not looking at the sky

next year my master
will walk the moon

120

we walk the neighbourhood for hours
windows filled with
mah-jong, cocktails, sitcoms
the face of Buzz Aldrin

no dog has walked the moon

121

what falls from the sky
teeth
priestmonks
car parts
toothpaste
famous Bulgarian hairdressers
famous Congolese hairdressers
Brylcreem
string quartets
dog smiles
missiles
turds
Knight from B4 to Q7—check
John F. Kennedy immersing himself in state secrets
matchsticks
cheese
walnut tables
the ancient and honorable order of bassoonists
the ancient and honorable order

Laika

122

John F. Kennedy and Laika
assassinated in the month of November
3 years apart

Joe Frazier, heart a burlap sack
bob, weave, left hook, repeat

Jupiter ballistic missile tango
Spanish bombs in the Lorca disco

123

earth is like trousers
oh, we call the earth
the pockets of a dog

we have our small hearts, large inside
where we hide everything else

124

ah yes,
large secrets
a dog whistle
a kingfisher
a feather
a life that comes
after this life

spacetime trousers?

I ask Happy, the trouserless dog, and he says a trouser is a spacetime model which a) can be divided, by means of two space sections $\Sigma\pm$ into three disjoint parts: the future of $\Sigma+$, the past of $\Sigma-$, and the rest, and such that b) $\Sigma+$ is connected whereas Σ_- consists of at least two connectivity components Σj with disjoint past, c) timelike geodesies meeting $\Sigma+$ meet Σ_- within a uniform interval of eigen time, and d) for each Σj there exists a timelike geodesic meeting both Σj and $\Sigma+$. This definition expresses what we understand by "uniting spaces". The lemma implies that such a world cannot exist: Choose $\Sigma+$ as the surface Σ from the lemma, and take for u^a a past directed timelike vector field such that in some points xj of $\Sigma+$, u^a agrees with the tangent of a geodesic meeting Σj. For sufficiently large s, the geodesic image Σ (s) must have swept past Σ_-, i.e. must have torn if the past of Σ_- was disconnected; which contradicts the lemma. Acknowledgements: Rex, Trixie. Oliver.

spacetime trousers?

the bad news is that there is no parachute
the good news is that there is no ground

126

nights on earth
dog and ghost
questions and answers

sometimes lucky
a spiral galaxy
29 million light-years away

127

poems as lichen
music an impossible fireswirl

$$\frac{n+1}{polka^{\infty}} \quad \text{—dimensional space}$$

ghost legs braided with dark matter

the multiverse hypothesis
a *compactified* beauty

while we dance to the music of 9 accordions

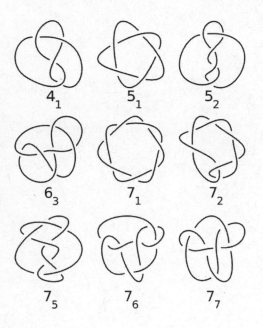

129

O let us return to my pet fungi
speeding down the highway
etymology: fungi's pronouns are "everywhere" and "entanglement"
whoooosh!

nothing like a fungi in a fast car
the braid of self a dream
my wife is ordering a dishwasher
his name is Martin

130

circle back to the kingdom of
yeasts and molds

desperate to name the nameless
long-chain polymer
tangle
schwamm
σφόγγος

the softness of the sound
self

131

a poem bends

)

a = b

(

i;f th;in;gs co;nsta;ntl;y cha;nge
h-ow ca-n th-er-e b-e th-ing-s?

132

the typo
while you were out
walking the dog
I was lost in the encyclopedia of cosmology
I, too, could hear the universe raging

133

I, too, typos
last night

you can put lipstick on a big bang
to bare withness

the wrong remains the sceme

134

typomancer
withness of spacetime

withoutness of horizon
a bend in the road
a broken

135

I was 8
Miss Devlin my teacher
explaining

there is a green hill far away
without a city wall

do you walk into the future or
does it come towards you?

time like an o

136

I was 8
red bandana, red star, white shirt
no priest, no minister, no telescope

ripple of years over a green sea
wheatfield in a jar

137

my grandfather's town so small
if you said its name
as you walked in
you'd have walked out
before you'd finished

Mark Twain said
those who are inclined to worry
have the widest selection in history

if the rich could hire
other people to die for them
the poor could make
a wonderful living

138

over my shoulder
geese and ducks and grandfathers
and even greatergrandfathers
clinging to their one copy
of Huckleberry Finn

139

mother
father
grandfather
grandmother
greats
great-greats
children
sons and daughters
there have always been
people dying for us

140

trajectory = a broken arc
lungs empty of ancestors

unknown birds
and grandparents

141

o yeah
that thing
yeast
fungi
lichen:
symbiosis
writing with you

    yes
    dear
        reader

the center will not hold
        yeast
        yeats

language biome

ink
        thinking

142

ink through the middle of thinking
and language

through the finite field
and how we said it together

143

the largest
island in the largest
lake on the largest
island in the largest
lake on the largest
island in the largest
lake in the world

we wouldn't be around to know
this is a beginning again

an unexplained crack in my tongue

144

to begin and begin and begin
in the middle of a sentence
after the final *yes*
of yesness

Acknowledgements

Thank You

To Michael Mirolla and the entire crew at Guernica for giving our exploding duck a place to land.

To Donato Mancini for his razor-sharp eye and wit. An editor who challenged and encouraged us, and helped us, yeastlike, to rise to the occasion, at every step.

To Rafael Chimicatti for the gorgeous cover design. We love the orange!

To our spouses and dogs and children, who first heard the explosion and believed.

About the Authors

Gary Barwin is a writer, performer and multimedia artist and the author of 29 books including *Nothing the Same, Everything Haunted: The Ballad of Motl the Cowboy* which won the Canadian Jewish Literary Award and *The Most Charming Creatures*, his most recent poetry collection. His national bestselling novel *Yiddish for Pirates* won the Leacock Medal for Humour and the Canadian Jewish Literary Award, was a finalist for the Governor General's Award for Fiction and the Scotiabank Giller Prize, and was long listed for Canada Reads. He lives in Hamilton, Ontario and at garybarwin.com

Lillian Nećakov is the author many chapbooks, including *The Lake Contains an Emergency Room* (Apt. 9 Press; shortlisted for the bpNichol Chapbook Award), as well as the full-length collections *il virus* (Anvil Press; shortlisted for the Pat Lowther Memorial Award), *Hooligans* (Mansfield Press), *The Bone Broker* (Mansfield Press), *Hat Trick* (Exile Editions), *Polaroids* (Coach House Books) and *The Sickbed of Dogs* (Wolsak and Wynn). Her new book, *Midnight Glossolalia,* a collaborative poetry collection with Scott Ferry and Lauren Scharhag, is forthcoming in 2023 from Meat for Tea Press. She has also published in many print and online journals in Canada and the U.S. Lillian lives in Toronto.

Printed in January 2023
by Gauvin Press,
Gatineau, Québec